T0036095

WHEN THE
COLOURS RUN

WHEN THE COLOURS RUN

lisa shatzky

Black Moss
Press
2015

Library and Archives Canada Cataloguing in Publication

Shatzky, Lisa, 1965-, author
    When the colours run / Lisa Shatzky.

Poems.
ISBN 978-0-88753-548-2 (paperback)

    I. Title.

PS8637.H378W44 2015   C811'.6   C2015-903876-6

Cover photo by Marty Gervais
Layout & design by Jay Rankin
Edited by Meghan Desjardins

Published by Black Moss Press at 2450 Byng Road, Windsor, Ontario, N8W 3E8. Canada. Black Moss books are distributed in Canada and the U.S. by Fitzhenry & Whiteside. All orders should be directed there.
    Fitzhenry & Whiteside
    195 Allstate Parkway
    Markham, ON
    L3R 4T8

Black Moss Press EST. 1969

Black Moss would like to acknowledge the generous financial support from both the Canada Council for the Arts and the Ontario Arts Council.

ONTARIO ARTS COUNCIL
CONSEIL DES ARTS DE L'ONTARIO
an Ontario government agency
un organisme du gouvernement de l'Ontario

Canada Council   Conseil des arts
for the Arts   du Canada

to my children — Jordyne, Benji, and Jonah — for the love
and laughter and joy each of you brings in so many ways to every
step of the journey,

to my beloved Don, who always knows where the poems
are and is the sailor who taught me to love the wind,

to that which creates life and breathes me awake and allows
me to write and sometimes even touch the sky,

thank you,
thank you.

CONTENTS

SECTION 1: WHAT YOU FIND IN THE DARK

SECTION 2: THE SOUND OF
THE BELL BEFORE IT RINGS

SECTION 3: WHAT BLOOMS

SECTION 1: WHAT YOU FIND IN THE DARK

"One does not become enlightened by imagining figures of light, but by making the darkness conscious"
—Carl Gustav Jung

WINTER'S QUESTIONS

And in the end
what will this have meant,
all this dancing and laughing, all this weeping

and starting over,
all this playing house and building mansions

and finding new places
and disappearing and reappearing
and saying forever
and changing our minds
then saying forever again,
what will it all have meant
at the end of our days
that we walked together sometimes holding hands
and diving into the depths of each other's eyes
and other times no longer in sight and

sometimes in opposite directions
each of us alone and each of us one of many.
I don't know the answer but once in a dream
it came to me like this:

each of our lifetimes were part of the same wave
we could not see it while in it but from a distance we were all
the same moment
of water rising out of the sea, the same force, the same source,

But wait, I don't know if it was a dream

or something I tell myself
so I can sleep at night
and imagine you are still here
that you did not leave

that your centre-stage smile and fire-lit eyes
are within reach
that all I have to do is look and you will be there
why just the other day I found a dried yellow rose laying

in the middle of the parking lot
and I picked it up perchance it was a sign from you
and just at that moment church bells rang out
and a fire siren sounded
blessing the moment of picking up the flower
making it a holy event
and the universe not random
and the question of what did it all mean
no longer important.

TINY WOUNDS

When the last wolf calls
to the mountain,
will you answer?

You remember innocence,
the Gaspe, the wildflowers, the sun,
summers when you brought your naked body
to the melody of clear brook water
to cool off and wash the salt from tiny wounds.
What you would have given to have stayed
forever in that light
and never left
and never known
the wolf you once saw
tied to the hood of an old Buick
eyes still open
surprised and amber and warm
legs splayed as if flying
white and black and magnificent.
And when they gathered
with their laughter and beer
and stories of the kill,
you thought you heard the wolf call,
unseen, unknown, impossible
but felt in the fabric of your skin.
Like a splinter that never came out
and the years grew over it
until one wolf became all wolves
and one child became all children
and falling became all falling

the leaves, the snow, the broken

and the road is littered
with children who fall and can't get up.
Eyes open and surprised
they grope, search for evidence
they're still here
and you hear them sometimes,
from the ashes and under collapsed bridges
and at the wailing walls.
You hear them from behind
locked doors and abandoned lives
and you know now
when the wolves call and the children weep
it is all the same song.

SUNSET KAYAK

Take me to the far edges
of what is known, then push me further
until frightened and awake I fall
into a purple yawning sky just to feel
your arms around me.

Kayak, vessel of sand and flame
my body, gold salt
we are one
dreaming of fish
huge moving fish through waters
below the surface.
(Sometimes I touch them. Sometimes they kiss my fingers.)

At dusk what we know
is reversed
slanted
elongated
such loveliness made of nothing.

Outbursts of rocks
and moss and islands
I have yet to explore.
The shadows of my shadow
spill themselves again in perfect
and diminishing light.
But the roaming moon

does not forget me.
A bright and bold kumquat
pouring in and I
can never resist.
Seals and starfish and blue herons,
forgive me for turning away.

Here in the oracle of darkness,
starlight is my only faith,
and the moon
my oldest lover.

WHEN THE COLOURS RUN OUT

What does it mean to be happy

a house with a view

a dog in the yard
pansies in the planter
where do you go with these
when the colours run out
when the jar is kicked over, by accident perhaps
when you are not looking
and you don't know how it happened
but all the blues and reds and oranges come
gushing out and the pinks and the pastels and all the soft shades
disappear
and what remains
turns hard and brittle and crusty
at the bottom of the jar
and the house with the view
can no longer keep the dog inside
who keeps escaping and digging holes
and climbing over the fence and shitting
in the neighbour's yard
and the house with the view no longer keeps you
warm at night
when you sit with your laptop
alone at the kitchen table
in the solace of the refrigerator
humming and whistling and rattling
as you struggle to find the lost melodies
of a story you think you once knew
the one where the boy and the girl
sleep through the night
in each other's arms
and give to each other
their breath.

WHEN THE COLOURS RUN

And then one day you realize
maybe years later
the colours never run out
even when the jars are kicked over
accidently (or was it intentionally)
and all the blues reds oranges yellows
come gushing or trickling out
they do not end,
not in the way you imagined.
When the colours run
it's because the sun changes directions
and the colours bleed into new rivers, oceans, volcanoes
even teardrops, raindrops
streaming down the glass.
And though you might still mourn the colour blue
for instance, what you thought was the purity of it,
do not mourn for too long
lest you miss the purple or indigo
blue becomes
for all the colours have their time in the sun.
Even when the sun disappears
the colours do not go
there is an ebb and there is a flow
all things being and becoming
moment to moment
from eye to breath and breath to light
and here you are —
the temple, the wonder, the breath, the sight.
So open your windows and open your doors
and do not fear the colours of night
for blue was never pure anyway, never innocent,
but always held a thousand shades of sea
and sometimes you must go where shadows go
and sometimes you must empty all your bags

and walk with nothing
and sometimes you must face the storm
lean into the exquisite wild wind
with your aloneness and emptiness
so you may dance again.
And when the light returns, (and it will),
notice how the geese also come back
even the daffodils push through the dark
every blade of grass sings
if you have the ears to hear it.
And all the colours return deeper and bolder
than ever before,
an orchestra of colours right at your feet
right where you stand
right here where the light pours into the room
like liquid gold, like oranges
imported from Spain
like warm kisses
on bare skin.
So just be still
hold quiet your longing anxious heart
for when the colours run,
they sing.

THE NAMES OF THINGS

I have no need for the names of things
so tell me not the Latin name for every flower
in the garden
for I shall not remember.
Instead speak to me of a thousand shades of red
how the red of strawberry explodes in the mouth
and the red of fire warms to the bone
and the red of your lips is a butterfly
dancing on the windowsill of my skin.
Then let us turn to the nuances of purple —
the fading sky in late August
a pail full of blueberries
that bruise on your arm
the sadness under your eyes —
then remind me of the miracles of green —
all those leaves and trees and newborn grass
holding the planet together
as we spin in orbits around what we think is real
only to learn later that nothing is as concrete
as we imagine.

So do not say *this is a table*
and *that is a chair*
because I was there when table was not table

but inquisition
and the little boy forced to sit with his plate

all through the night
because he would not eat his meat
until finally by morning gagging and sputtering
he was released
and sometimes that same table was a field

of land mines
and other times the table served silent nights
and cold wars
and on rare occasions the table was a fort
where the children gathered under it with their blankets to build walls

and huddled with their pillows
pretending they would never be found.
But that was long ago
and these days table simply means *offering*
the place where we eat and drink all the colours of the garden
and the sounds of laughter
more divine than wine
and perchance you wish to join me there
tell me not your name or from where you came
just show me what makes you sing
what makes you cry
how your heart puts itself back together when broken

and why.

IN OUR NEXT LIFE

In our next life when I call for you
will you come?
When our old dog dies in my arms
in the middle of the night
will you wake up when I call
and hold me tight?
And when the trees fall
all around the house
will you stay awake
and not turn away,
and if I call for you after midnight
because a wayward bat is flying lost and confused
in the airtight woodstove that no longer holds fire
in our kitchen
will you not let the bat die
knowing I can hear its screams
even if it does not scream
I can hear it
I can hear it suffocating
will you love me enough
to care for the midnight bat flying helter skelter
in the woodstove that has no fire
in our kitchen
like our marriage
around and around in circles we flew
smashing into the glass again and again
while life carried on
as if nothing
was wrong
and when we finally looked up
the bat
was gone.

MUTILATION OF THE THIGHS

The moment he calls you
to tell you his wife is leaving him
because his hands on her thighs
repulse her
is the moment you feel shame
for belonging to the gender
that commits hate crimes
against thighs.

You remember watching her
in the kitchen many years ago
as she prepared the chicken
for the barbeque. She held a beautiful
oversized knife that gleamed in the afternoon
sun reflecting the outside canopy
of delicate leaves and pink and white
pansies in the planter box. With hard jabs
she got the chicken thighs into position
and made neat little lacerations
along the edges with counter-clockwise
gashes becoming longer and stronger
with each turn until every last inch
of fat was identified. Then she let loose
slashing vigorously and gleefully,
oblivious that you were still in the room.
Meat and skin came flying off
in all directions including some skin
from her thumb but she carried on
as if nothing was wrong.
Blood splashed onto the chicken,
down her hand, and into the salad bowl
of mixed baby greens.

You rushed to get a towel
but she just laughed and said it was no big deal
as she tossed the salad into the garbage
and continued the mutilation of the thighs.

This was the first time
you became afraid
for him.

ANOREXIA

Arched fingers dance on ribs in rhythmic counting rituals

spaces in between bones

bones in between spaces

vover and under and over again.
Hunger is no longer hunger
but a hiding place
the blanket you wrap yourself in
to deny the outstretched arms of night.
Eyes once turquoise lakes
now decaying midnight pits
where nothing blooms.
Under the barren sky of stomach
eating itself one morsel at a time
the planets have fallen and the stars
have burned the mysteries the wildflowers
the golden suns all obliterated.
This is the celebration of disappearance.
Not a disorder but a monster
the kind that used to live in the closet
when you were small and afraid of the dark.
Now it is out
erasing your name
devouring your eyes
leaving you longing and aching for more.
Where are you where are you
friends ask.
You can hear them
but can't find your way out
of the mouth's gasping empty hallway
where all the words used to live.
Their shredded and starved remains

make croaking sounds
but no one understands them
not even you.

WINGS

I wanted to write a collection about the girl
who killed herself.
I wanted to wade through the swamplands
of her thoughts,
bushwhack the hidden trails
of her soul,
untangle the knotted strings
tightening her heart,
but I could tread no further
than her face.
She was eighteen and she threw herself from a bridge
in the middle of the night.
I saw it but had no way to stop her.
No time to tell her
that when living hurts
the heart still carries on
beating its tiny wings against the caged night
and even when the song appears to be gone
it is only hiding behind midnight clouds
and summer will return
and the moon will spill its white heat
all over the strawberries in the garden
and things with wings
can be heard everywhere.
Had I been able to touch this girl
her desert eyes and half-life smile
her rough hands and delicate body
I might have said:

butterflies, dragonflies, fireflies
hummingbirds, robins' eggs
bare feet on fresh cut grass
sweet corn peaches plums
moonrise after summer thunder.

EARTH CALL (1)

Do not turn away.
I wasn't always the old lady on the street
corner with her hand out,
scorched skin
and hollow veins
waiting for you.
It is not time but appetite
that created such barrenness,
your appetite
relentless and thrusting
hot and thirsting into every possibility,
every small opening,
every newborn green,
leaving a feverish trail
of cultivated mutilation.
I know you yearn for me as I was,
painted in green abundance,
flowing rivers wild
and making love to a gentle sun.
Under the tired depleted surface I am
still here, see the forest breaking
up the pavement,
one shoot at a time.
Make no mistake about it,
I will return,
make a comeback
fierce and unequivocal
like the weather, not an anomaly
but a response
to your calling
for me
as I once
was.

EARTH CALL (2)

At some point she will come for you,

because you called,
she will reach for your hands
and lead you to wander
the overgrown trail near the cemetery,
through wild lavender and spilling foxgloves,
through tricky thorns and furrowed earth
because you dreamed
of painting outside
the lines.
But will you follow her
across the river's precarious edges
and hot sands and jagged skulls of stones?
Will you climb the cookie-crumbling gravestones
with names of the fallen
and will you dig up all the things
you longed to say but didn't? Will you
pull the aching silences from their burning
crevices and caress them with trembling reverent
hands and wipe the oily shadows
from their pores and breathe them
back to life?
She will come for you
because after the rain
what else but the memory of the sun beams
to lead us back into the forest?
And she will whisper colours you have not
yet imagined. But imagination
can take you only so far.
Eventually you must learn to paint,
paint with long and embellished sweeps
to howl back the mountains again,
to swim in the rivers and weep

in the arms of great trees,
and only then will you
touch and taste and love more
than what you have
become.

NOW THAT GLOBAL WARMING IS MAINSTREAM

Some days it's better not to read newspapers,
to choose to go without
glancing at headlines
from across the bus.
If even for only one day
I wish to be oblivious
to the growing list of calamities
and apocalyptic potions
and twelve-step programs
on how to go green.
Now that global warming is mainstream
and has slipped from the hands
of the naysayer-vegan-tree-hugger types
to join ranks with crimes against humanity,
there are no safe places left to hide,
or so they'd have you believe.

Maybe I'll just forget newspapers entirely
and sit by the fire and read Al Purdy
poems and have him tell me once again
about the rooms for rent in the outer planets.
I'm sorry to take you so literally
dear Al whom I will never know
except for that one time when
at seventeen I crashed
my way into a Montreal after-hours pub
to hear you polishing your stories
by the midnight hours. I don't remember
what you said except for the way
your thin shrewd lips sliced the words
carefully, to feed to me slowly,
until begging and aching I reached
for more.

I still savour those intonations.
I imagine where you'd place the comma.

But what I really want to know
about those rooms for rent in the outer planets
is how to reserve one
in case I find myself trapped one day,
in a cabin on a runaway train
with windows cemented shut and the floor caving in
and being the procrastinator that I am
it wouldn't surprise me in the least if
just as we were headed over the cliff
I'd suddenly wonder if I had made that reservation
or if it was still on my to-do list

but of course it would be too late then
so I'm enquiring now:
where shall I make a reservation
and can I have a room with no view please?
You see, I don't want to see
the stars and the moon. As lovely
as they are, they would remind me
of my life on Earth and what I really want
is to forget, just for a moment,
to be caught up in something so wildly delicious
and out of this world
that I may grow wings and become
a great song flying through the Milky Way,
a little lost, a little not here,
just for a little while.

WHAT YOU FIND IN THE DARK

If your spirituality leads you
to the mouth of the cave
then you must go inside
and light a candle by which to see
and go deeper
to find that which is speaking to you
through the dark.

But if what you find in the dark
becomes your refuge
your ghetto
your wailing wall
and you dedicate yourself
to rearranging the tables and chairs
and justifying the doors
and building more walls

then be aware that butterflies can not find you there
and colours will fade and songs
of the wind will die
and you will not hear when the butterflies cry.

But if what you find in the dark
leads you to an alpine meadow
where the view is long and wide
and wildflowers dance unabashedly
in the sun and when it rains
even the trees bend and bow
in prayer and the mountain
trembles but still there is moonrise
after the thunder
and music in the trenches
and communion without walls

then you will have found
a way of being
free.

SECTION 2: THE SOUND OF THE BELL BEFORE IT RINGS

"If you want to awaken all of humanity, then awaken all of yourself. If you want to eliminate the suffering in the world, then eliminate all that is dark and negative in yourself."
—Wang Fou, Huahujing

THE LANTERN

You find yourself again
in a forest at midnight
and come across an old lantern by the pond.
You have been here a hundred times
and still can go no farther.
Midnight and a lantern that does not work.
How many times must you come here
before the illusion of the lantern
wears off? Or the truth of its essence
revealed: the lantern never worked
and never will.
But you thought if you danced long and hard enough
before the murky pond
and made pledges to the lantern in the dark
and tried on different faces
and took off your clothes
and let yourself be cold
and trusted the waiting
and stood among the thistles and the thorns
and gave yourself to the wind,
the lantern would light.
It did not.
And yet here you are again,
hands cold and no more disguises.
Even the old stories you tell
about the lantern don't work.
Even the lies.
And you could stand here forever
for there are many ways to die
or you could let the moon back in
for a brighter and bolder sky
and permit yourself the glory of the stars
so you may turn away from the lantern

and find again your life.

WAITING FOR YOUR PSA SCORE

The pin prick. The blood taken.
A few days to find out if the doberman
has come back to the door or if it's still in remission.
In these days of waiting
between the pin prick and the call to the doctor,
I make promises to the moon
or G-d, depending on the day, promises
to be a better person, one who rises at 4:00 am
to do daily meditations and prayers on a cold wooden floor
with a shawl wrapped around my shoulders
and a begging bowl and a small bell.
I don't know why there is a bell.
But it is always there.
I am my best in these days.
In between the pin prick and the doctor's call,
I become a white wolf guarding an old wolf
through the secular night.
I become a fierce wind bending and bowing the trees
until the sun bleeds back the day.
I become a moment plucked from the whole,
the tear drop on your face,
the blue bird landing on the broken veranda
at the back door,
waiting, waiting

believing

in spring.

PRETENDING TO BE A POET

Sitting at an outdoor cafe   and pretending to be a poet
what I mean is I sit here   with my pen and paper
at a small table under a maple tree in the village
and I do not write.
Instead I watch all the people walk by
as if caught in a current, a steady flow   of back and forth
they come and go   movement upon movement
    this life force of which I am part
    this moving into and stepping away
this being part of something
and sitting at this table   pen and paper in hand
and wanting to say something about the people   or myself
or the movement or what I see or   don't see
and not knowing where to begin   except with a question
    the one I think we are all asking
though don't ask me what it is   because on most days I can't remember
but it sounds like the bell of an old cathedral
or maybe it is the sound of a tree frog
    I can't tell the difference anymore
but there is a question   we are all asking
maybe it is the first sigh when awakening in the mornings
as the light   first enters your room
or maybe it is the sound a turtle makes when it dies
a long melodic yearning sound
or something like that
but even longer.

THAWING TIME

Just because the pond is frozen
doesn't mean it is dead.
You keep forgetting that part.
You think the freezing means
all those things below the surface have disappeared.
And for a while all is well.
You skate on the surface
doing figure eights
and blowing bubbles as you chomp your gum
and the day is bright and the ice glistens.
But whatever is was that was rising to the surface
before the freezing
is still there
suspended in time.
How easy to forget.
How easy to stay on the shiny surface.
But spring is coming
and there will be a thawing time
and whatever age you were
when you first froze over,
that little you,
will rise again
with that look in her eyes
her heart in her mouth
and a knife in her hands.
Wanting to feel something
for the first time in years.

LEARNING TO SWIM

Just because the boat floats
doesn't mean it is going anywhere.
You have known this for some time
but you stay with the boat anyway
because yesterday the sun was warm
and the boat brought you to new islands
hidden inlets, and green
and lush forests.
Today the boat hovers ever so slightly
on the water
like a bubble, fragile, alone
and you stand on guard for the holes.
New holes appear every day
and you plug them up one by one
and count your blessings the boat is still here,
even if the engine rusted over
years ago and the sails
could never withstand the wind.
Off in the distance
there are new waves, waterfalls,
hot pearls of sand
where the turtles are waking up.
You can almost hear them.
One day you will be asked to decide
between a life of holes
or learning to swim.

COME INSIDE

If you want to come inside,
take off the armour
and open the door.
Or, we could stand here on the porch for a while.
It's pleasant after all, and the door mats match the flower pots
and there is a hummingbird feeder by the window
and we could talk about the weather, how autumn is coming
you could tell me again about the new barbecue you purchased
how it is so big it could grill a whole cow if you wanted to
and I will nod politely and refrain from mentioning I am a vegetarian
and maybe we will laugh a little and then you will say you have to go
(as you always do at this point)
and I will ask you again to come inside before the day gets cold
and the years disappear
and you will laugh and say there's still lots of time
but I hear the clock ticking and summer is gone
and I remember the boy who laughed when the cow jumped
over the moon and hey diddle diddle
what can I do but meet you in the middle
you won't come inside
so we live on the porch
where we have lived for years
but it gets cold here
and sometimes there is not enough to eat
yet I touch your shiny armour with my small hands anyway
and tell you it's beautiful
because I know it pleases you
and still I long for the days of the living room
when you came inside
and took off the layers
and we sat by fire
and shared a few of our favourite verses
and exposed our naked hearts
and were made whole again.

LEARNING TO TALK

Her voice, a storm, an angry shrill
of tsunami undercurrents
hoarse wild waves
exploding between boulders
dead crab sea kelp algae
making a mess of things again

his voice, a gentler wind
in the late afternoon
as clear as vodka
as solid as ice
something to stay warm with
when the storm returns
(and it will, it will return)

the youngest voice, a flyaway kite
the string is gone and wings are broken
but it still flies helter skelter
higher and higher away from this scene
we can barely make out the colours anymore

my voice, the dark of moon
hiding
behind shattered clouds

and we are learning to talk.

WHAT WE SAY WE WANT

Some of us know what we want
right from the beginning
and some of us never know

but something in us is always moving,
even in our grief,
even with our heavy hearts,
even when the sky is falling,
we cross new frontiers
into tomorrow and we want everything
even when we say
we don't.
Or maybe
it is simpler than that.
Maybe we wake up in the mornings
and we purposefully do not ask G-d to keep us
away from trouble
because we already know that trouble
is part of the human trip
and it does not worry us
as much as the thought
of missing something.
If we ask for anything at all,
if we pray at all,
perhaps it is simply to not miss anything.
Perhaps we ask to be spared from nonchalance,
spared from cynicism,
spared from a missed opportunity to kiss,
to weep in another's arms.

And though words will never be enough
if we had to choose just one word,
it would be   yes, yes
to love unrequited, undeserved,

to every sunrise
birdsong
smile
touch
yes to the seasons, the unending seasons,
the complicated and glorious and painful seasons
all of them, yes, yes.

TYPES OF MEN

Fire men light up the sky and burn from within.
Their intensity and electric heat draw you closer
and like shooting stars they transport you
to new universes
while still living on earth
in a state of perpetual fire.

Earth men live closer to the ground.
They like getting their hands dirty
digging and building and making a mess of things
creating beauty from nothing.

Water men can go anywhere.
They are easygoing and bubbly
can take the shape of anything
fit into any container, any hole, any home
be whatever you want them to be.

Air men float and drift and are as open as the sky.
They live amongst the outer planets
and sometimes the moon
and don't need much of anything
just a few galaxies and infinite time
for their endless projects and plans
that never get finished.

And all the types have their gifts —
water is sustenance
air is space
earth is roots
fire is heat
but fire begets fires
fire longs for more fire
its hot tongues recite burning poetry

that causes the back seats of cars to light up
in smoke
and what is a fire girl to do?
Air men may ignite the flames
but can not hold the heat
and water men extinguish the fire
as they were born to do
and earth men glorify dirt and dark and worms
a little too much
and fire simply stands alone
ablaze
lightning
a burning bush
and oh what delight to kiss a burning bush
to hold the flames and not be burned
but the real trick for a fire woman
who chooses to be with a fire man
is how to stay alive
without burning down the forest.

HOW TO CATCH A BUTTERFLY

If a butterfly suddenly comes into your life
and lands in your open hand
know the glory of its wings
is for you.
But do not cup your hands over it
do not give it a name, nor build it a box
and adorn it with gold.
Never carve your initials in the soft pale of its flight
and tell the world it belongs to you
for the butterfly must fly
must know the ecstasy of wind and sky
the delirium of the seasons
or it will die.

Instead you must keep your hands open

allow the butterfly to quiver every inch
of your body in song,
kiss your lips with its wings,
its tiny heartbeats the echoes
for your laughing and longing.
And the butterfly will dream the music
it brings from your bones
become the colour of your heart
when your heart learns to fly
be the reason you breathe
the reason you cry.

SOME THINGS TO CONSIDER, OR
WHAT I HAVE LEARNED SO FAR...

If you wander from room to room
in the house you think you know
with a single candle in one hand
and eagle feathers in the other,
waxing ceremony and magic and pretending
you're from another era,
you will indeed discover
rooms you never knew.

Rather than invent more legends of the dark,
now is the time to light as many candles as you can find.
Get drunk on the words of Basho
and Rilke and watch how the shadows
then bless the walls.

Start a lover's quarrel for the sake of some sparks.

Take off the handcuffs you put on years ago.

Stick your neck out
the window and listen for the soft
humming of moth wings
in their search for more light.
See them as they really are,
the forgotten poets
praising the night.

Open wide your doors to the lost
alley cats and other creatures
for they will come skulking
from all corners and gather
in the tiny hours.
See your own

longing in their eyes
for a little grace now
is what will keep you
warm
later.

For when it comes right down
to it, when the light falters, inevitably
fails, and all ideologies and intentions
and politics go up in smoke
and you find yourself in the quiet
still of impending darkness

all you will have is love
and prayer.

THE PROBLEM WITH POETS IS...

They spend so much time staring out the window and then complain they have no time to write.

They warn us to open our eyes and slow down
and not let life pass us by
and yet they can spend an entire day deciding on where a comma goes
and consider that a good day's work.
They believe that in a poem something lost can be found again
yet most of the time they can not find their keys, their glasses,
where they are going, when they last did their laundry, or that one great
indelible poem that has the answer to an exceedingly important question
that is no longer remembered.

THE SOUND OF THE BELL BEFORE IT RINGS

You are awake and the day begins
the sun slowly breaks through
the birds in their winter-is-almost-coming frenzy of wings
and you are up early because you crave
contact with the silence
your need is to touch and taste the moment of pause
before the next thing happens
the sound of the bell before it rings
you sit blurry eyed on the floor of a small cabin
your son sleeping
in the next room
for a moment he is still young
and you are in privilege
to his needs
the sky yawns pink and gold
the old cat pushes up against you
as if in prayer
and the moon lingers from last night's dreams
which you do not remember
for a moment not a sound
only the sensual choral refrains of your heart
rising and falling
like rain, like mist, petals to the wind
here, here, here
and your answer,   your only possible answer
thank you, thank you.

SECTION 3: WHAT BLOOMS

"If you bring forth what is within you,
what you bring forth will save you.
If you do not bring forth what is within you,
what you do not bring forth
will destroy you."
  —The Gospel According to Thomas

WHEN THE BUTTERFLIES CRY

She sits drawing circles
while I stir the spaghetti sauce,
purple green yellow circles
like bubbles, floating, not touching
across a white page.

Why do butterflies have so many colours? she asks,
not looking at me.
What? My mind is blank
like the whiteness of her page
and the sauce is starting to burn.

The butterflies! She sighs loudly and asks again.
I don't know, I smile,
but I am far away, lost,
wanting to be carried away by one of those
buoyant circles,
light, bright
untouched
floating off
the whiteness.

I suppose, I try on the mother hat again,
I suppose they're made that way.
It's weak. Unimaginative.
But it's the best I've got today.
The well is dried up. In fact,
there is no well,
only an un-well,
a sick feeling thickening
at the bottom,
like the spaghetti sauce
now sticking to the pot.

What is evil? She is chewing the top of her felt
pen again, even though I have asked her a million times
not to. Well, maybe not a million.
A small detail in the scheme of things.
The radio has been off for days
but she remembers.
Perhaps we all do,
even when we forget.

Evil, I would like to answer, *is when people crash planes
into buildings on purpose.*
Instead I say, *evil is when the colours disappear. When there is only
black and white.*
Oh, she says, *when the colours disappear
do the butterflies cry?*
I don't know, I mumble.
She draws big circles now.
Pink, orange, blue, yellow
all the colours of her crayons
she makes bigger and bigger circles
touching all the smaller circles and soon all the circles are joined.
All connected. As if holding hands.
My escape plan of floating away
in a solitary circle has come to an end
and so, by the way,
has the spaghetti sauce.

She continues to draw circles on top of circles
on top of more circles with more and more colours.
What does it all mean? I ask,
scraping out the pot.

They're butterflies. Her voice is matter of fact.
*Butterflies dancing in the wind.
To bring back the colours, see?
That's why they're made, see?*

Yes, I do.
I see.
How right
she is.

THE CROWS ARE FORNICATING

The crows are fornicating
by the side of the road
in between the drive-thrus
and the dry cleaners
amidst the traffic and the noise
the crows are there
on the small parcel of grass
that remains in the tongueless streets
one on top of the other
black wings flapping like broken kites
on the ground.
The crows are fornicating
as if nothing else matters
as if the world might come to an end
unconcerned about those stuck on buses watching
unmoved by the motion and commotion
by the affairs of man
the crows carry on
proclaiming yes to the open polluted sky
yes to the sun trying to break through
yes to life longing for itself
yes to the moment
yes to the day.

WHAT MATTERS

What matters is that you do not pretend
you do not hear the water's ancient melody
over stones in the river
and you do not turn away from the questions
ringing inside you like bells in the monks' hands.
What matters is that you do not ignore the alpine meadows
and their wildflowers singing the cobalt sky
and you say yes to the laughter
and yes to the tears
and you open yourself up to the mountain
so the sun can find you
and the wind can caress your face
and the grass can kiss your feet.
What matters is that you say yes to the dance
and yes to the songs
yes to the night and all its stars
yes to the colours painted by light
yes to the deserts and their longings for soul.
What matters is that you say yes
to the voice inside the voice
of the one you forgot
the one who dreamed
and played and loved
and you bring forth
what is in you
to bring forth
and you break through your own walls
and erase your own ceilings
and stumble and fall
and get up again
as you find your way
home.

DIGGING

These days I dig to plant seeds.
Or create something.
When I was small I learned
the only way to survive was to dig
holes to hide in,
trenches to defend myself in,
and long dark tunnels for which to plan my escape.
But now the digging is all about thriving.
So when you say, bring me a pail
sometimes I like to throw myself inside it,
hoping you will notice how nicely I can conform
to the shape of things when I want to.
Instead you focus on the water splashing
over the sides and making a mess of things
and ask if the pail is big enough.
Well let me tell you, my darling, the pail will never be big enough
for all we must carry.
Our conversation then changes to shovels and pails
and sometimes they are one and the same
for the thing that is buried is also still carried
and what is carried
on some days
also carries us.
It's hard to know which came first.
But when your eyes fill with tears
and your pail is overflowing
do not fear
for I am by right your side
and I become the warm sea
where a thousand newborn fish
have made their home in me.

SPRING POETRY

Whatever else it is,
it must be ravenous,
picking clean every cold
morsel, thirsting out of every nook
and rock and moment
to defy the outstretched
arms of night. Skunk cabbage
in baroque green exploding
in drowsy creeks. In the city
it is warm enough for the homeless
to return. Scrambled grasshopper
dragonfly mosquito tree frog songs
make a comeback
despite the odds.
And spring cleaning in the suburbs
means a doll with no eyes
a stroller with one wheel
and a bright white mattress
are left by the side of the road.
The city planners plant
marigolds and other pretty things.
But the old temple
where the cherry blossoms grow
is waiting demolition.
Sometimes I go there
to weep.
Dimpled rain is
caught on newborn petals.
Spring is what survives.

IF I COULD FRENCH KISS YOU

If I could French kiss you
the way those Quebec boys taught me
in my youth, my tongue searching the sailor's
wide ocean of your mouth, and if I could be
sure it would not lead to anything
beyond the moment, that you would not be left
wanting something more or need it to be real
or that you would not ask to meet me
by the river's edge where the sun
makes love to the water, and if I could be
sure you would not want to cover every inch
of my skin with your lips and that you would not
ask for this exploding summer delight to last
through winter's long inevitable grip
or you would not expect moonlit
walks where our bodies come together
like music, like colours, like sound,

if I knew for certain you would not ask
for anything more,
then yes, yes, I would, I would.
I would kiss you as if it was
the last day of my life.
But I don't trust you,
not even for a second.
Nor do I trust myself.

IF YOU SAY YOU LOVE ME

then do not speak to me about the moon and stars
and how the earth changed directions on its axis
when we first met
for what I want is closer to the ground.
I want to know if we crashed down hard enough
the doors to each other's hearts,
if the walls were shattered,
and if the ceilings came down,
and tell me, was there any blood?
I want to know what you dream of
when you wake up
in the middle of the night
with tears in your eyes
asking if I still love you.
I want the real story, the uncensored version,
how love is messy and foolish
and does not keep a ledger,
how love waits up all night in the cold and rain,
is sleep deprived, crazy, and more hungry than wise.
If you say you love me
then tell me again about the kiss you waited for
your whole life,
tell me about longing and wildfires
and things being burned to the ground,
how love breaks us again and again
so we may become more whole.
If you say you love me
tell me how love
was the catastrophe
we did not plan,
that grabbed us by the throats
and brought us back
kicking and screaming
to life.

BIRTHDAY WISHES

This year for my birthday,
I simply want you to spray-paint all the walls
all around town
with dirty and profound graffiti
in all my favourite colours
purple burgundy gold.
Then let's find a place
where we can walk forever
without knowing where we are going
only the open spaces to guide us
and a sense of the wind
and the fragile forgiveness of the seasons
and may we laugh and laugh and laugh
even when there are tears.

JUST TO SAY

I did not recover from losing you,
nor did I become clever or savvy
on the subject of loss,
nor attend any groups on how to
walk with serenity or equanimity
or other attributes I can not even name.
Instead my ears and eyes
grew keener
and everything lost
was found again.
A letter you wrote slips
out of a recipe book I was
about to recycle and when I wander
through the night-blooming orchids,
your voice follows like an eager moon.
The paperweight with the owl head
you brought back from Inuvik
sits on my desk with its wide
charcoal eyes from the other
world. (Did I mention I am in love
with owls these days? How they come to me,
calling in the midnight hours?)
And your etchings of Japanese horses
sometimes leap out of their paper lives
and enter my dreams
and yes, I admit I ride them shamelessly to other planets
and for a moment, there too,
trees rattle and leaves hum
the sound of your name to the sun.
The other day I lay on the earth
after the rain (a habit you
never approved of)
to watch the sky beckon
the night and the old cat

with the blue eyes crawled
onto my chest and wouldn't leave.
I didn't mind the purring but
there's only so much raw-meat
cat breath one can take
so I nudged him off, but each time
he returned more tenacious
than the last and I finally gave up,
thinking maybe he was a part of you.
I swear I heard you laughing just then.
Something about too much sentimentality.
Indeed I did not recover
from losing you.
Everything lost
is found again.

SUMMER FRAGMENTS

Finding the blackberries you missed.
Being kissed by the sun
everywhere.
The moment
is fire
gold sweat
heat rising
outdoor cafés.
Everything is burning orange,
becoming what it already is.
Nothing withholds
nothing waits
red salmon pink indigo violet blue green.
A lone teenage boy with hands in his pockets
follows a laughing cluster of cackling girls,
tough beautiful girls cracking their gum
and their heels as if they own the world
and pretending they don't see him.
(He will follow them forever and they will glance
over their shoulders to make sure he's still there.)
A moon sliver meets the setting sun.
Children scream barefoot in the grass.
Lawn mowers purr suburban along the edges.
Cats coo ecstasy in the midnight hours.
Noise bylaws can't be enforced.
And all those blackberries, oh those blackberries,
the ones you missed
found again.
Your insatiable hunger for the sea,
that cold blue beckoning of salt water
like the delight of a lover
never quite possessed.

WHAT AM I

but a falling dew drop,   a rising mist,   a waterfall.

A forgotten song, the missing key.

The door ajar, an untuned guitar.
What am I but light on water, a bubble
on the surface, appearing, disappearing.
Reappearing. One leftover leaf.
A plastic bag.
Caught in the wind.
Caught in the song.
Flying leaves   and falling light.
What am I but an empty boat,
the newborn fish under the hull.
The algae and barnacles and seaweed
kissing the rudder, holding the keel.
The waiting crabs on the ocean floor.
Singing leaves and dancing light.
The wind, the plastic bag
flying high above the boat,   above the mists
over waterfalls and sudden songs,
missing keys and open doors.
The plastic bag made beautiful.
What am I
but the newborn light.

GIFTED

It is when you think
or when you claim
that these long glorious white violet
shimmering silver blue diamond days
and nights of summer's abundance
unbidden and undeserved
belong to you
that the crickets will hesitate
and the wind will no longer call
your name.
So make no assumptions.
It is all a gift.
There on the placid lake
a bubble is catching holding reflecting
a thousand shades of light
born of the morning
dust.
The broken shells
under the bigleaf maples
where blue herons made their nests
are what you leave
behind.
If you are lucky,
the grass will sing
your praise.

A HUNDRED YEARS

I watch you sleep in the early morning
and know the moment to be beautiful
the moment of everything that is here
the cat sleeping on your chest
the gulls doing their morning incantations
the light dancing the room
the temporary moment
one after another
is what makes up our life.

Soon the moment will change
the coffee machine will make its gurgling
sounds and the smell of strong java
will follow and the cat will rise and fall
as your breath becomes heavier.
The light will waltz to another room
the phone will ring
someone will need something.

Then the cat will leave your chest
and you will ask how long I have been up
and I will wonder what I actually did
while you were asleep
and that too will be a moment.
I will tell you I thought about a family member
I have not spoken to in a year
she disappeared without telling us
where she was going

and you will share this moment of pause with me
and maybe put your hand on my shoulder
before moving on to the bathroom
and I will notice the slight stiffness
in your morning walk

and your old sailor's hands
as they brush against mine.

Then the geese will move on to somewhere else
and the gulls will replace them
and we will say good morning again
you will pour the coffee
I will stare out the window
and more moments will come.

If I can remember a hundred moments
at the end of each day
who is to say
I did not live
a hundred years?

WHAT BLOOMS

It is spring
and the skunk cabbage is back
with its baroque green boldness thrusting
through the mud
its damp earth shit smell everywhere
on trails and in gutters
along streams and roads
there is the skunk cabbage
with its in-your-face here-ness.
and up-your-nose audacity.
You think this is the season of butterflies
and songbirds and things with wings that sing
but the skunk cabbage always comes first
more daring than beautiful
rising out of its own death.
Leaves curled and furled like fists
it makes its way through the blackness
until slowly opening
to a yellow bloom in the middle
pulsing with heat and possibility.

Somewhere in you is that same boldness
to push through the dark,
to rise out of the hurts and the falls
to climb out of the murky swamplands
and the lost trails of you,
to wipe clean the grime and ass of you
to bend and break the scars of you
until you find another you
and slowly you open yourself up
like the flutter of petals

like moth wings to the light
and maybe if you are lucky
maybe
something
will bloom.

ACKNOWLEDGEMENTS

I am deeply grateful to Marty Gervais, publisher of Black Moss Press, for his ongoing belief and support of my work over the years. I also thank Meghan Desjardins for her keen eyes and attention to detail in the editing of this collection. I wish to also thank Jay Rankin for the vibrant and artistic cover to the book that captures so nicely the many cadences of when the colours run. I thank all the magazines and journals and chapbooks that have published so many of my poems, many of which appear in this book. And of course I have gratitude for the readers and lovers of poetry. Without you, there would be no point. For poetry is one soul speaking to another soul. Come inside.

ABOUT THE AUTHOR

Lisa Shatzky's poetry has been published in *The Vancouver Review*, *Room Magazine*, *Quills Canadian Poetry Magazine*, *The Nashwaak Review*, *The Antigonish Review*, *The Dalhousie Review*, *Canadian Literature*, *Canadian Woman Studies*, *The Prairie Journal*, *Jones Av.*, *Grain*, *The New Quarterly*, *Monday's Poem*, and six chapbooks by Leaf Press (edited by Patrick Lane) along with anthologies across Canada and the US. Her poetry book *Blame it on the Moon* was published by Black Moss Press in 2013 and was shortlisted for the 2014 Acorn Plantos Award for People's Poetry. Her poetry book *Do Not Call Me By My Name*, also published by Black Moss Press (2011), was shortlisted for the Gerald Lampert Poetry Award in 2012. Shatzky has also had prose published in *Living Artfully: Reflections from the Far West Coast* (Key Publishing, 2012) as well as poetry in *This Island We Celebrate*, published by the Bowen Island Arts Council in 2013.

When not writing she runs marathons as a way of meditation and works as a psychotherapist on Bowen Island, BC, where she lives on a boat with her partner Don, her teenagers, a dog called Sherman, and three cats.